Wonder

Contents

OXFORD
UNIVERSITY PRESS

Great Clarendon Street, Oxford OX2 6DP

Oxford University Press is a department of the University of Oxford. It furthers the University's objective of excellence in research, scholarship, and education by publishing worldwide in

Oxford New York

Auckland Cape Town Dar es Salaam Hong Kong Karachi Kuala Lumpur Madrid Melbourne Mexico City Nairobi New Delhi Shanghai Taipei Toronto

With offices in

Argentina Austria Brazil Chile Czech Republic France Greece Guatemala Hungary Italy Japan South Korea Poland Portugal Singapore Switzerland Thailand Turkey Ukraine Vietnam

Oxford is a registered trade mark of Oxford University Press in the UK and in certain other countries

First published 2013

British Library Cataloguing in Publication Data

Data available

ISBN 978-019-839102-9

10 9 8 7 6 5

Printed in China by Printplus

Acknowledgements

The publisher and author would like to thank the following for their permission to reproduce photographs and other copyright material:

cover: © Tad Carpenter; p3: R.J. Palacio; p4: Used by permission of The Random House Group Limited; p5l: Used by permission of The Random House Group Limited; p5m: From *Wonder* by R.J. Palacio, published by Doubleday. Used by permission of The Random House Group Limited; p5r: Tad Carpenter; p9: Peter Barritt/Alamy

Illustrations by Steve Evans.

A Letter from R.J. Palacio

Dear Reader,

About five years ago I took my kids to visit a friend of mine, and at some point during the day we found ourselves sitting next to a little girl who looked the way Auggie looks. My younger son was only three at the time, and he reacted exactly the way you might think a three-year-old would react when seeing something that scared him: he started to cry. And though my older son, who was ten, knew better than to stare, his expression said it all despite his best efforts: he looked like someone had just punched him. It was terrible and I got up as quickly as I could to remove us from the scene – not for their sakes, of course, but to spare the little girl's feelings. As I pushed my younger son's stroller away I heard the little girl's mom say, in a calm voice: 'Okay, guys, I think it's time to go.' And that just got to me.

On the drive home I couldn't stop thinking about how that scene had played out. It occurred to me that they probably went through something like that dozens of times a day. What would that be like? How could I teach my children to respond better? All this stuff was flying through my head on the car ride home. After a while I turned on the radio just to keep myself from thinking about it and the first thing that started to play was Natalie Merchant's *Wonder*. It was so amazing because that song had always been one of my favourites – but that night the words really hit me. It was like the song had been written for this girl I had just seen.

The book kind of wrote itself in my head on that drive home. I would write the story from the child's point of view. It would help people understand – not pity. 'I'm just like you,' the child would say. 'I'm an ordinary kid – except for this one thing.' And I would call the book *Wonder* because this child is a wonder.

If anyone who reads *Wonder* can relate to how Auggie feels, they might think twice before saying something thoughtless about someone different from them. I'm hoping they'll find a character they can relate to. It might make them rethink who they are. Are you more like Jack or more like Julian? Are you Summer or Charlotte? If a kid like Auggie were in your class, how would you treat him?

R.J. Palacio

Judging a Book by its Cover

No matter how good a book is, the right cover can make all the difference between it becoming a best-seller or being left on the shelf.

The author of *Wonder*, R.J. Palacio, also works as a cover designer and so she had very specific ideas about what she wanted for the cover of her novel; she said that she wanted the cover to have 'humanity and edge'. There were lots of sketches in the planning process before the final cover designs were chosen.

Look at one of the early cover designs opposite.

What do you think about this sketch? Do you like it? Do you prefer the cover on your version of the novel? In small groups, discuss:

- what this cover tells you about the story
- what you like about this version of the cover
- what you dislike about this version.

Now read the author's feedback about this cover design in an email to her editor:

Send | Save | Attach | Fonts

From R.J. Palacio

To Editor

Subject 'Wonder' cover

I'm all for simplicity and being graphic and abstract, but it's the style I am having a big problem with, unfortunately. The **iconography** of the face is almost a little sign-like, which makes it a bit **generic**-seeming and certainly very cold. And because it's so crisply drawn, it's misleading: the face in these is perfectly proportioned. It's also young-seeming. I'm afraid this little boy could be the hero of any book about any 10-year-old kid (he looks more like seven here)—there's no sense of something being off-kilter.

Conceptually you're right on the money, I think. But I ask that you please ask [the designer] to give it another go-around with his sketchy doodle style PLEASE. Let him do an outline of a face with his beautiful irregular quirky black line, where the ears are slightly off, and the WONDER-type encircling the eye is like it is in the single-eye image. It would be an amazing cover.

generic – not specific
iconography – use of images and symbols in art

Judging a Book by its Cover

A

B

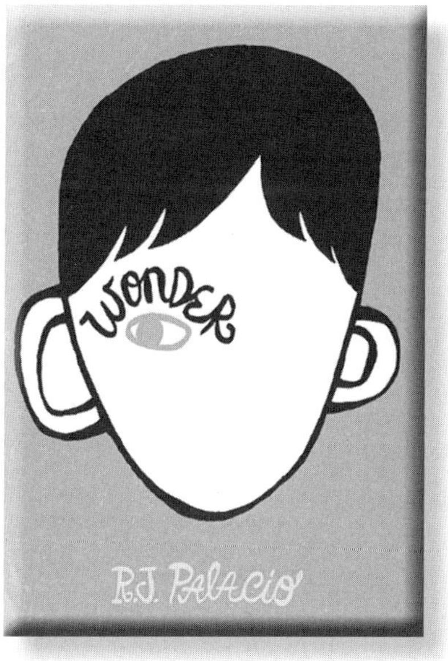

C

In pairs, look at these three book covers. Each one was produced as a possible design for *Wonder*. Can you work out which cover was designed for a children's edition of the novel, which one was designed for adults and which option was ultimately rejected by the author? Give reasons for your decisions. You should consider:

- the graphics and images used
- the font used
- the choice of text
- how these elements might appeal to the target audience.

Tagline

Look at the **tagline** for the book, which is included on the front and back covers of some editions of the novel. A tagline is a kind of slogan or memorable phrase that is used in advertising.

> Don't judge a ~~book~~ boy by ~~its cover~~ his face

- What does this tagline reveal about the book? Make some predictions about the story.
- Does the tagline make you want to read the book? Why, or why not?

Your Wish is My Command!

From the beginning of *Wonder*, we are told that the main character, August, has a facial disfigurement. August tells the reader that if he found a magic lamp he would wish for 'a normal face that no one ever noticed at all'.

> 'I won't describe what I look like. Whatever you're thinking, it's probably worse.'
> – August

In small groups, think about some of the other characters in the novel. While none of them faces the same challenges as August, the writer makes it clear that these characters also have obstacles to overcome.

What do you think each of the following characters would wish for if they had a magic lamp?

- Via
- Jack
- Summer
- Justin
- Mrs Pullman (August's mum)
- Mr Browne

Give reasons for your answers.

What would you do?

Imagine you have the magic lamp and you are allowed one wish. What would you wish for? Would you wish for something for yourself or would you wish for something to help someone else?

Draw a picture of the lamp in your exercise books, with a bubble emerging from the spout (like above). In the bubble, write your wish and explain your choice. Consider:

- how the wish will affect your life or someone else's
- what life is like without the wish being granted.

Now present your idea in front of the class. Speak clearly and be prepared to answer questions at the end.

Unfamiliar Words

American English

August lives in New York in the United States of America. The story is written in English but there are lots of words, spellings and phrases that we don't use in Britain, such as: 'schlep', 'jack-o-lantern', 'fifth grade', 'dude', 'Mom' and 'homeroom'.

Keep a log in the back of your book of all the unfamiliar words and phrases used in *Wonder*. Look up the words in a dictionary or online and add the definitions to your log.

Quotations

The writer, R.J. Palacio, uses a quotation from a book or song at the start of each section of the book, when the **narrator** changes. Keep a list of the quotations and explain why you think each one is relevant to that part of the story or to a particular character.

Choose three chapters/events from the book that appeal to you or that you found particularly powerful. You might consider 'The Bleeding Scream' when August overhears Jack being unkind about him to Julian; 'Alien' when August is attacked in the woods; or 'Floating' when he's given an award by Mr Tushman.

Create a table like the one below and select a quotation from a book, poem or song that you think has some meaning to the events in the chapter. Be ready to explain your choices!

narrator – the person in the novel who tells the story to the reader

Chapter title	What happens	My quotation	Why I chose it
'Alien'	August is attacked by older boys in the woods on a school trip.		

First Impressions

Think back to your first day at secondary school. Did you make friends easily? August receives a mixed reaction from other students when he starts his new school: some, like Charlotte and Summer, are kind and friendly; Julian, however, is very cruel.

From the beginning, there are narrative clues to hint that Julian is going to be difficult. We learn about characters from what they say, the way they behave, how they look and what others say about them. Copy the table below and add to it as you gather more information about Julian.

Page number	Quotation	What it tells us about Julian
p28	'forced a smile'	He doesn't want to be there and is pretending to be friendly.
p30	'he didn't look at me once while he talked'	He's rude and seems to have an issue with August's appearance.

Think of three questions that you would like to ask either Charlotte or Julian about their first meeting with August. Ask two people in your class to play Julian and Charlotte in a **hot-seating** activity. The rest of the class should ask questions.

Diary entry

Write a diary entry for either Charlotte or Julian after they meet August at school for the first time. What would they really think about the new boy with the strange face?

Remember, when writing a diary entry you should use the first person ('I'), write mainly in the past tense and include information about the character's feelings. You can also use slang words!

For example, Charlotte might write:

Met a new kid today. He seemed quite sweet but I couldn't look at him much as he had a really weird face. I feel sorry for him...

Or Julian might write:

Our school is like a freak show nowadays. I had to show an alien where to go – the ugliest kid I've ever seen. Gonna be fun to push him around...

The Worst Best Day

Re-read 'The Bleeding Scream', which describes what happens when August arrives at school on Halloween. How does the reader know that August is upset by what he overhears in this chapter?

Copy the table below and explain the effect of each quotation. The first one has been done for you.

Quotation	Effect
'I knew the shrug… I knew the voice… I knew I wanted to run out…'	The repetition of 'I knew' shows that August has realized that it is Jack talking. The fact he repeats it suggests it had a great impact on him.
'My face felt like it was on fire'	
'The tears were so thick in my eyes I could barely see'	
'I wanted a hole I could fall inside of'	

Costumes

August's Halloween mask is based on a famous painting, *The Scream*. How might the image in the painting reflect his feelings at this point? Explain.

In pairs or small groups, think about what other kinds of costume are included in the novel and what their purpose is; for example:

- August's astronaut helmet – why does August wear it? How do his family feel about it and why?
- Julian's Darth Sidious costume – why does Julian decide to wear this costume? What does it tell us about his character?

Now think about less obvious kinds of costume in *Wonder*. Do any characters wear 'masks' so that other characters can't tell what they are feeling? Think about:

- August's mum
- Via
- Mrs G and her 'shiny smile'.

You've Got a Friend in Me

We all value our friends but what do we like about them? Brainstorm all the qualities you think make a good friend.

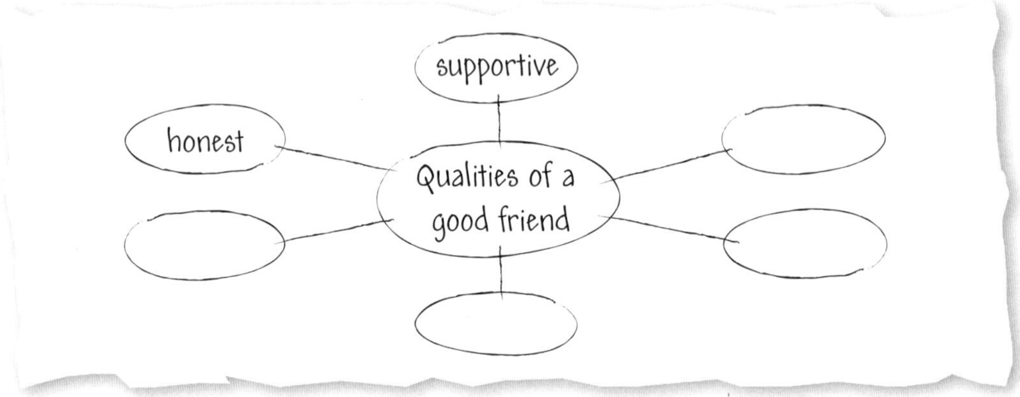

How many characters in the book show the qualities of a good friend in your opinion?

Shifting loyalties

Miles, Henry and Amos fall out with August and Jack because of Julian. However, later in the novel, the boys help August and Jack escape from the bullying boys in the woods.

Hot-seat the character of Miles. Try to find out why he suddenly stood up for August and helped him out of a difficult situation. You could ask questions such as:

- Why did you decide to turn against Jack and August in the first place?
- How do you feel about the way you behaved?

Betrayal

Friends sometimes make bad decisions – we are human after all! Can you think of a time when you let a friend down or when someone let you down? Look again at the two incidents in the book where August and Via felt betrayed by the friends they trusted: Jack, Miranda and Ella.

Get into groups of two or three and improvise a scene in which August or Via confront their 'betrayers' with their feelings.

- What do you think they would say to one another?
- How would the 'betrayers' react if they knew August's or Via's true feelings?

Remember, your aim is to mend the friendships!

What about Me?

Re-read Via's version of events in Part 2. Note down all of the difficulties that she faces, such as coping with August's condition, starting a new school and losing her best friends.

'So much for the old movies and mother and daughter bonding.'
– Via

Now read this imaginary letter from Via to an agony aunt, asking for advice to help with her problems:

Dear Agony Aunt

I hope you can help me. My brother has a genetic condition that means he has a really serious facial disfigurement. Everyone stares at him and some people make nasty comments – I hate that and I get so angry that I can't make life easier for him.

I sound mean saying this, but Mom and Dad spend so much time caring for Auggie and making sure he's okay that there's not very much time left for me. My face may be 'normal' but I still have problems. My best friend seems to have ditched me over the holidays and practically ignores me. I want things back to how they were before. Since my lovely Grans died, there's nobody who puts me first.

I'm 15 now and will be an adult soon. The doctors have told me that any baby I might have has a 50/50 chance of looking like Auggie.

Please give me some advice as life is pretty miserable for me right now.

Olivia

Imagine that you are the agony aunt. Write a response to Via's letter. What advice could you give to Via to help her deal with some of her problems?

Dear Olivia

Thank you for writing to me. I'm sorry to hear that you are so unhappy – what a lot you have gone through…

Different Perspectives

The novel is narrated by several characters. Each character has a different view of events. Why do you think that the writer chose to write the book in this way?

Match these extracts from the novel with the character that you think is talking.

'But hey, if they want to give me a medal for being me, that's okay. I'll take it. I didn't destroy a Death Star or anything like that, but I did just get through fifth grade.'

'i'm not used to all the attention, to be truthful. my parents don't have a clue about what I want to do with my life. they never ask.'

'And this is the way it's always been for me, for the little universe of us. But this year there seems to be a shift in the cosmos.'

'I hate science the most out of all my classes. We get so much work it's not even funny!'

August | Jack | Justin | Via

- How did you know which character was speaking?
- How does the author create a distinct voice for each character?

Adult viewpoints

We never hear directly from the adults in *Wonder*. Choose one of the following adult characters from the story and write a monologue from his or her point of view. Don't try to cover all events in the novel, but pick out two or three key moments and tell them from the adult's perspective.

August's mum

Mr Tushman

August's dad

Reading between the Lines

In the chapter 'Letters, emails, Facebook, texts', Julian's mother, Mrs Albans, emails Mr Tushman after Jack and Julian's fight. She writes in a formal manner, selecting her words carefully for effect, but what does Julian's mum really think about August?

Send | Save | Attach | Fonts

From Mrs Albans

To Mr Tushman

Subject Jack Will

... To that end, I wonder if Jack's unexpectedly violent behavior might have been a result of too much pressure being placed on his young shoulders? I am speaking specifically of the new child with special needs who both Jack and Julian were asked to 'befriend'. In retrospect, and having now seen the child in question at various school functions and in the class pictures, I think it may have been too much to ask of our children... There are many parents – myself included – who question the decision to let this child into our school at all.

Imagine Mrs Albans is talking to a close friend about the situation. How do you think she would talk and act then? What would she say? In pairs, role-play a conversation between the two about Julian, Jack and August.

When you have finished your role-play, write a script for the conversation between Mrs Albans and her friend. Set out your script as below but feel free to change the words:

Mrs Albans: I can't believe dear Julian is having to sit in every lesson with that 'boy'. My poor baby says he can't concentrate at all as the boy's grotesque face is so off-putting. No one can eat lunch with him in the room – how upsetting is that?

Friend: Oh, how awful for Julian.

Mrs Albans: What are his parents thinking? There's obviously something wrong with them anyway...

Your Deeds are Your Monuments

August's English teacher, Mr Browne, gives his students a monthly precept in his class. A precept is a rule or motto. Mr Browne describes it as 'anything that helps guide us when making decisions about really important things'.

One of Mr Browne's most important precepts is:

YOUR DEEDS ARE YOUR MONUMENTS.

- Make a list of all the good things you have done in your life. Include small things like babysitting your little sister or making your mum a cup of tea, and big things like raising money for charity or working hard for an exam.
- Write your list onto coloured pieces of paper, using a different piece of paper for each good thing on your list. Be as artistic as you like!
- Create your own monument of your good deeds. You could make your deeds into a colourful collage, adding drawings or photos to make it more interesting. You could even make it three-dimensional using papier-mâché!

Whenever you feel miserable or unimportant, look at your monument and know how special you are!

> Look around your classroom. Without speaking, pick out someone in the room who isn't one of your close friends and who you don't usually talk to. On a sticky note, secretly write their name and something positive about them.
>
> As you leave the lesson, put your note on the door. Your teacher can make a list of all the positive comments for the class to see when you come into your next English lesson.

Sanjeet:
He's brilliant at maths.

Sarah K:
She really supports her friends.

David:
His art is amazing!

Becky:
She is so funny.

Your Deeds are Your Monuments

During the graduation ceremony, Mr Tushman quotes from J.M. Barrie's story *The Little White Bird*. He picks out the line: 'Always try to be a little kinder than is necessary.'

In a pair, discuss what you think he means by this:

- How can you be kinder than necessary?
- What words of wisdom have your parents and/or grandparents given you?

Precepts

In the appendix at the very end of the book, Mr Browne's precepts are listed and those written by some of his students. Why do you think the author chose to end the novel in this way?

> Pick one of the precepts at the back of the book. Write a short morality tale where the final line of the story is your chosen precept.

Self-portraits

Think about what values are important to you: family, trust, friendship, loyalty, courage, kindness, etc.

Design your own postcard precept. Draw a self-portrait on the front and then write your own personal precept on the back. You can either make your precept up or use a quotation that you found somewhere. Your precept should be something that has real meaning to you.

Create a class display of your postcards and all the values that you hold.

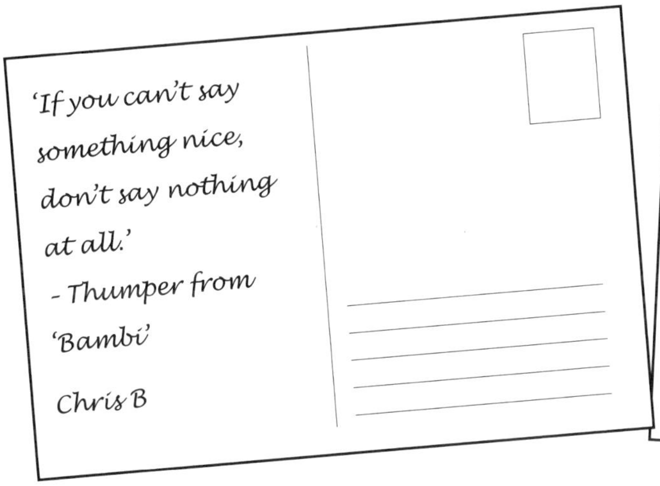

Pathways... to Another Good Read

Books about outsiders

The Curious Incident of the Dog in the Night-time by Mark Haddon
ISBN: 978 009 945025 2
Teenage narrator Christopher has Asperger syndrome. He understands maths and science but struggles to work out other human beings. When he finds his neighbour's dog lying dead he decides to track down the killer and write a murder mystery novel about it. In doing so, he discovers other secrets that threaten his whole world.

The London Eye Mystery by Siobhan Dowd
ISBN: 978 019 832900 8
Ted and Kat watch their cousin Salim get on board the London Eye. But after half an hour it stops and everyone troops off – no Salim. Where could he have gone? How on Earth could he have disappeared? Ted, a boy with autism, and his older sister, Kat, start to investigate the mystery. Ultimately, it comes down to Ted to find the answers.

Mortal Engines by Philip Reeve
ISBN: 978 043 997943 6
An adventure story, set in a fantastical world, featuring the facially disfigured Hester, who doesn't let her disfigurement get in the way of what she wants.

Stargirl by Jerry Spinelli
ISBN: 978 184 616599 3
When she arrives at the local high school, Stargirl is determined to be herself. She's different from the other kids – she just acts herself. But can the rest of the school put up with someone so different?

The Skin I'm In by Sharon Flake
ISBN: 978 019 832675 5
Maleeka suffers from the taunts of the other kids about her home-made clothes, her good grades at school, and her dark, black skin. When a new teacher, whose face is blotched with a startling white patch, starts at their school, Maleeka predicts trouble. But Miss Saunders loves the skin she's in.
Can Maleeka too?

Books about bullying and prejudice

The Edge by Alan Gibbons
ISBN: 978 184 255094 6
The boy in this story excels in sports, and it is this talent, together with his reunion with his grandparents, which help him and his mother through their struggle to escape his mother's bullying, abusive partner.

My Sister Lives on the Mantelpiece by Annabel Pitcher
ISBN: 978 019 913728 2
Ten-year-old Jamie Matthews has just moved to the Lake District with his dad and his teenage sister, Jasmine, for a 'Fresh New Start'. Five years ago his sister's twin, Rose, was blown up by a terrorist bomb. His parents are wrecked by their grief but, to Jamie, Rose is just a distant memory. Jamie is far more interested in his cat, Roger, his birthday Spiderman T-shirt, and in keeping his new friend Sunya a secret from his dad.

Noughts & Crosses by Malorie Blackman
ISBN: 978 019 832861 2
Callum is a nought – a second-class citizen in a world run by the ruling Crosses. Sephy is a Cross, daughter of one of the most powerful men in the country. In their world, noughts and Crosses simply don't mix. Can Callum and Sephy find a way to be together? They are determined to try. And then the bomb explodes…

Starseeker by Tim Bowler
ISBN: 978 019 832890 2
Luke is still coming to terms with the death of his father when he finds himself the target of a notorious gang at his school. He has a choice: join them by breaking into a house to prove his worth or stand up to them and become their latest victim. Skin, the leader of the gang, is violent and unforgiving, but Luke is willing to risk everything to protect a precious secret.